TISSUE PAPER CRAFT

TISSUE PAPER CRAFT

Richard Slade

FABER AND FABER
24 Russell Square
London

First published in 1968
by Faber and Faber Limited
24 Russell Square London WC1
Printed in Great Britain by
Latimer Trend & Co Ltd Whitstable

S.B.N. 571 08306 4

CONTENTS

Introduction   *page* 11

1. Materials and Tools   13

2. Cut-outs   15

3. Prints   19

4. Collages   22

5. Flowers   29

6. Use of Tissue Paper with Waxed Paper   37

7. Simple Models   39

8. Constructions   41

9. Mobiles   44

10. Moulded Objects from Ready-made
    Articles   47

11. Moulded Objects from Own Moulds   51

12. Scrolls   57

13. Other Uses for Tissue Paper   60

ILLUSTRATIONS

Photographs

1. Cut-outs   *page* 16
2. Potato printing   19
3. Potato prints   21
4. Flat, abstract collage   23
5. Flat, representational collage 26
6. Raised, abstract collage   27
7. Raised, representational collage 28
8. Flowers   31
9. Jewellery   34
10. Mounted flower piece   35
11. Simple models   40
12. Constructions   42
13. Mobiles   45
14. Mobile and waxed paper hanging 46
15. Modelling over balloons   48
16. Clown's head and small figure 49
17. Modelling over own moulds   51
18. Puppet head and masks   52
19. Making piñatas   54
20. Finished piñatas   55
21. Scrolls   58

Diagrams

1. Design samples for rectangular cut-outs 15
2. An aid to drawing margins   17

9

3. Method of pasting tissue squares for collages *page* 22
4. Method of making enlargements   25
5. Flower shapes (1)   29
6. Flower shapes (2)   33
7. Circular cut-outs   38
8. Method of pasting tissue paper on plasticine
      model   52

INTRODUCTION

The basic materials for this craft are simple and inexpensive. The results are often surprisingly beautiful. Tissue paper of various tints and paste are the essentials.

When you have made a few of the things described in this book, you will find that the craft is one that lends itself to originality. This is especially true with regard to collages and constructions.

The handling of the delicate and colourful paper is almost certain to awaken your creative powers.

1. MATERIALS AND TOOLS

The advantages of tissue paper for certain kinds of work have led artists to experiment with this medium. Some forms of papier mâché craftwork, for example, are much easier, more accurate, lighter and stronger, when tissue paper is used. The Japanese have long been aware of this, and the lightweight paper, not unlike tissue paper, which they employ for some of their papier mâché work has enabled them to produce articles of great durability and charm.

Tissue paper has much to recommend it in the decorative field. Very pleasant wall decorations can be made quite easily. Because the medium is inexpensive, these decorations may be discarded and replaced as often as desired. This is true of flower work: classrooms and libraries benefit from an occasional spot of bright colour, and this may be readily achieved by having a small bowl of tissue paper flowers on a desk or shelf, flowers which can be changed often with a minimum of effort and outlay.

Tissue paper in a wide variety of colours can usually be bought in large stationery shops. Should you have difficulty in obtaining it, Dryads, Northgates, Leicester, carry stocks, and no doubt a postcard to them would bring you a list of the colours supplied.

Almost any kind of paste may be used, but different types of paste are sometimes better for different jobs. For some kinds of work, starch makes an excellent adhesive. It is ideal for flat collages and papier mâché work.

Obtain the lump starch. Put two tablespoonsful into a two-pint basin, add a tablespoon or two of cold water and mix it into a thick paste. Pour a pint and a half of boiling water (it must be boiling) on to this and stir. When this is cold, you have a good, clean paste which can be thinned down if necessary.

When working with starch, pour a small quantity into a handy container, such as a saucer. If you use a brush, let it be a soft, flat one, and wash this free of starch when stopping work.

Cellulose paste is also a very good, thin paste. It is usually sold in small packets, and a teaspoonful to a pound jam jar of water is about right.

A library paste, such as Gripfix, is better for raised collages and flower making. For some articles, a little tube glue is necessary.

It is as well to have a large piece of plywood or hardboard to work on when occupied with papier mâché. This will eliminate unnecessary mess, and it can be quickly washed down afterwards.

You will need a large, and maybe a small pair of scissors.

A twenty-four inch or longer ruler is very helpful for measuring wall space and for frames.

While the centre of a frame may be cut away with scissors, you will make a neater job with a straight-edge and a craft tool or similar handicraft knife. This type of knife is also useful when you make constructions and mobiles. So, too, is a pair of long-nose pliers, small size.

Other tools will be mentioned as the need for them may occur.

Other materials which may enter into tissue paper work are reed, balsa or cork, wire and card.

Paints and brushes will, of course, be necessary for finishing some models.

2. CUT-OUTS

These are very easy to make, but they are an effective means of decoration.

Take a piece of tissue paper 18″ × 12″ of the colour of your choice. Fold it five times, dividing it into equal halves each time, to make thirty-two divisions as shown in the diagram. Keep it folded.

Now cut pieces out of the folded tissue, as indicated in the diagram. A card template may be made and the cuts made round this as a guide. Open out the tissue and you have a pattern which can be mounted on tinted card.

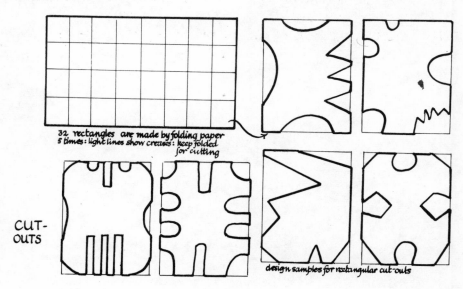

32 rectangles are made by folding paper 5 times: light lines show creases: keep folded for cutting

CUT-OUTS

design samples for rectangular cut-outs

1. Design samples for rectangular cut-outs

Pay attention to colour harmony, when mounting the tissue. Mount light green tissue on dark green card, violet on mauve, orange on yellow, and so on.

A dab of paste will keep the corners of the tissue in place.

1. Rectangular and circular cut-outs

16

A white frame of card will enhance the pattern and make a pleasant wall decoration.

Card Frames

These are made from white card according to the size of the pattern. For the above size of tissue paper, the width of the frame should be at least three inches.

Place the frame card on a flat surface and, using a piece of card 3″ × 3″, mark off the three inch width in each corner, as shown in the diagram. Join these points with ruler and pencil. Cut away the unwanted centre-piece.

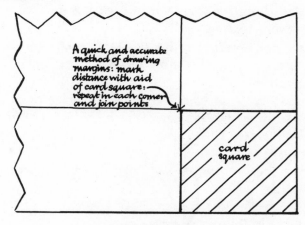

A quick and accurate method of drawing margins: mark distance with aid of card square: repeat in each corner and join points

card square

2. An aid to drawing margins

If you use scissors for removing the unwanted card, first pierce the centre of the card, cut diagonally to each marked corner and cut along the pencil lines.

A neater job is made by cutting away the waste card with a craft tool. Lay the card on top of some sheets of newspaper on a flat surface. Place a straight-edge along the line to be cut. Hold the straight-edge firmly and cut towards you with the knife.

Using the same method, you can cut frames to any desired size. You might also like to experiment with frames of various shapes.

Wooden Frames

If these are used, place them over the white card frame to leave a white margin between the tissue and the wood.

An empty space on an exhibition stand can be made attractive by using these patterns in an unmounted series. A colour harmony can be used for this. Colour harmonies are composed of like colours, e.g., red, orange and yellow, or blue, turquoise and green. Classroom walls also take on an added interest with this form of decoration.

Experiment further with other folds and cuttings to create different patterns. In order not to waste tissue paper, you can first experiment with newspaper cut to the desired shape and size. When you have achieved a pattern in this way which pleases you, refold the paper to show how you made the cut-outs. This can then be traced on the folded tissue with a soft pencil, or you can hold the design as a template against the tissue and cut round it.

Some suggested designs are shown in the diagrams, but these should only serve to get you started.

When making a cut-out pattern of this kind, take care how you cut the edges of the paper or you may find the paper cut into several pieces instead into a pattern.

There are many ways of using these cut-outs for decorative effects. They will, for example, add an air of festivity at a children's party, if placed over a tablecloth. Using smaller sizes, you can make table mats as settings for dishes.

Small cut-outs can be covered with clear plastic material as settings for vases and bowls.

Experiment with various paper shapes, such as circles, triangles, pentagons and so on, folding them as previously.

3. PRINTS

It is rather difficult to achieve good results by painting with a brush directly on to a sheet of tissue paper, but it accepts a printing stamp very well.

The easiest and perhaps most attractive form of printing on tissue paper is potato printing.

Place the tissue to be printed on a flat surface over a few layers of newspaper.

2. Potato printing: method of making print

On one side have another small pad of newspaper and your paints. Poster or tempera colours give good results: the tempera should be mixed with a little thin paste, starch for preference.

Take a fairly large potato, clean it and slice it evenly in half. A sharp kitchen knife is best for this. Slice off parts of the sides of one of the halves to form a more or less rectangular shape at the cut end, and this will be the base of your printing stamp.

Cut a simple design on this base.

Brush some paint on to the small pad of newspaper. This is your printing pad, and the top sheets can be discarded as necessary.

Press the potato stamp on the pad and practise printing a few times on a spare piece of paper, until you are satisfied with the effect.

Press the potato down firmly and lift it cleanly to avoid smudging: you may have to hold the tissue in place. Do not try to make good with a brush or by overprinting those parts of the print which may be fainter than others. The attractiveness of potato printing depends largely on the unevenness of texture in the printing.

When you are satisfied that the potato stamp is working well, apply it evenly over the whole of the tissue. Judge the spacing by eye: do not measure it with a ruler.

A finished print can be a repetition of just one design and colour, or of two or more designs and colours. If you wish to overprint the first slightly with another, make certain that the first print is quite dry.

The potato can be cleaned or made ready for another design by taking a slice off the printing side.

Many interesting patterns can be made with potato printing, and tissue paper has the advantage over other types of paper for this work in that its own texture greatly enhances that of the print.

These can be framed like the cut-outs.

A development of this idea will be found under the heading of 'Scrolls'.

Other forms of printing, carried out basically as for potato printing, are achieved by using stamps made from other suitable vegetables with a texture similar to that of a potato, or from rubber.

When cutting a vegetable to obtain a working base, use a sharp knife with a long blade. This helps to keep the surface flat and even. Work on the base can be done with a penknife.

3. Potato prints: showing finished prints and reed made ready for making a tissue and reed mobile

4. COLLAGES

These can be two or three dimensional, in other words flat or raised. Or they may be a combination of both. They can also be abstract or representational, that is, a pattern or a picture.

The measurements are a matter of choice. It is best, at least in the initial stages of experiment, to work on card or paper about 25″ × 20″. This allows freedom of movement. If you intend to frame this with a three-inch wide frame of the same measurements, then draw a margin a little less than the width of the frame around the card or paper and confine the picture to the area made by this margin.

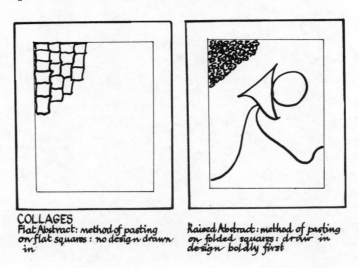

COLLAGES
Flat Abstract: method of pasting on flat squares: no design drawn in

Raised Abstract: method of pasting on folded squares: draw in design boldly first

3. Method of pasting tissue squares for collages

A Flat, Abstract Collage

On a piece of thin card or a piece of strong paper, such as cartridge paper, paste various pieces of tissue paper as follows:

First cut or tear some tissue paper into pieces about one inch square.

22

4. A flat, abstract collage

Have an assortment of colours. These can be kept separate in box lids, or put out in separate lots.

When you have a good supply, arrange them on the card, working methodically from side to side, or from top to bottom. Fasten the tissue in place as you proceed with starch or other thin paste, varying the colours according to your judgement of harmony and contrast. A small amount of contrast will be more striking than a lot. For example, if you are working in harmonies of blue and green, a tiny splash of red adds a nice accent.

Overlap the pieces as you paste them down.

The final result will be a pleasant abstract pattern rather like a tachiste painting.

Experiment can be made with shapes other than squares. For example, try circles and triangles. Small card templates of circles and triangles can be made and held against several thicknesses of tissue paper for cutting out.

A Flat, Representational Collage

Take a sheet of thin card or strong paper and a colour photograph or picture. The outline of the picture has to be transferred to the card, and this is done as follows.

Make guide lines on the card to correspond with guide lines on the picture.

First divide the picture into four rectangular quarters, then draw the diagonals across the picture and in each of the quarters. If necessary, the division can be carried out in each quarter as for the whole.

Divide the card in the same manner. The diagram should make all this clear.

Using the lines as you guide, copy the picture, drawing in only the essential outlines.

Cut or tear small pieces of tissue paper of the colours required and fill in the outlines by pasting on the tissue pieces.

When this collage is dry, an added emphasis can be given by going over the outline with a dark blue crayon or paint.

A Raised, Abstract Collage

You will need a sheet of card or paper as for the previous collages. If you wish, an abstract design can be drawn on this.

Tear or cut various colours of tissue into pieces about an inch square. Fold each small square into four, that is two folds, one each way.

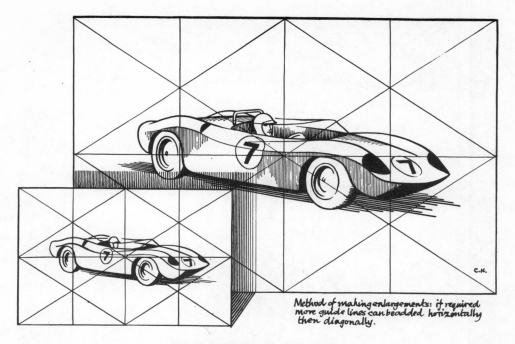

Method of making enlargements: if required more guide lines can be added horizontally then diagonally.

4. Method of making enlargements

The tissue is fastened to the card by flattening the closed corner of the folded tissue, and pasting it on to the card. Use a white paste, such as Gripfix.

Fill up the card with folded tissue squares. Work methodically, keep the tissues close together and arrange the colours in pleasing groups. If a design outline is drawn, the names of the colours forming parts of the design can be written in the appropriate places beforehand. To speed up the work, small areas can first be covered with paste and the tissue pressed into place on this.

Press down lightly on the tissue, when the whole of the card has been covered and the paste is dry.

Variations on this can be made by using circles instead of squares; by cutting various edges; by working with larger units of tissue.

Colourful textural effects can be achieved with this abstract pattern work, which will look well when placed in a wooden frame. Leave a margin of white card between the wood and the tissue.

5. A flat, representational collage

6. A raised, abstract collage

A Raised, Representational Collage

Tissue is prepared as for the raised, abstract collage. The work is first carried out as for the flat, representational collage, using a picture and drawing in guide lines. The tissue is then stuck on the card with white paste.

All these collages look well in a frame. Instructions for framing will. be found under the heading of 'Cut-outs'.

7. A raised, representational collage

5. FLOWERS

The use of crêpe paper for the making of flowers has long been well known. Tissue paper has not been greatly used: different and delicate effects can be achieved with this medium.

There should be no effort to make exact copies of flowers; the aim is to create a pleasing and colourful decoration, not replicas. The original flower should be, so to speak, a starting point for our creativity.

Independent Flowers

By this is meant flowers which can be made singly and used as dress ornaments or placed in bowls or vases.

The first requirement is a template. A number of shapes have been set out in the accompanying diagrams from which a stock of templates for different flowers can be made.

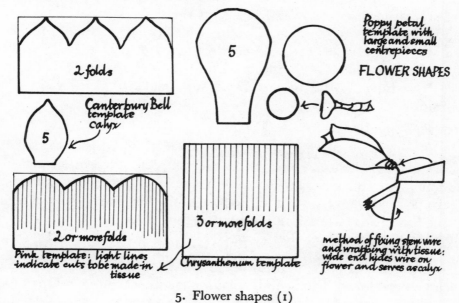

5. Flower shapes (1)

Thin wire is also needed for the stems. A roll of thin galvanised wire is very suitable.

White paste is more efficient for this work.

Cut a number of pieces of tissue paper of the required colour a little larger than the template of the flower you intend to make. Take about six of these pieces, lay them one on the other and cover them with the template. In this way several petals can be cut out at the same time. Cut round the template.

Arrange the petals into the shape of the flower, twist the base of the petals together and fasten the petals at their base with thin wire. Let the wire be long enough to form a stem: if the wire is very thin, allow enough for it to be doubled back on itself in order to make a stronger stem.

Wrap the stem wire with a strip of green tissue. First fasten one end of the strip to the base of the flower with paste to serve as a calyx. After winding, finish by pasting the loose end. The diagram will help to make this clear.

Sepals, if necessary, can be made from small pieces of brown tissue cut to size and shape.

To curl the edges of a flower petal roll it round a pencil, knitting needle or something similar.

I have set out some flowers for your guidance: many others can be made on the same principle. The size of the flowers is not important. You can even create flowers of your own. Try, for example, making eight very large rose petals. Assemble these and curl the edges. Use any colour you like for the petals. You will find that a few of these large, rose-type flowers in a suitable vase make a pleasing form of decoration.

Chrysanthemum

Fold a piece of coloured tissue paper 9″ × 3″ lengthwise to make a square 3″ × 3″. Cut as indicated in the template diagram. Open out the folds and roll fairly loosely. Put a touch of paste at the base to secure. Wrap stem wire around the base of the flower and open out the petals. Finish with green tissue around stem wire.

Pink

Fold a piece of pink or white tissue paper 8″ × 2″ in two to make a rectangle 4″ × 2″. Cut as indicated for the pink template. Open fold and roll. Secure the base with paste, and add stem wire. Open out petals and wrap green tissue around wire.

8. Flowers from tissue paper

Rose

Cut about seven petals of one colour, using the small rose template. Arrange the petals to form nearly opposite pairs: the first pair rolled fairly closely and fashioned to form the centre of flower, and the others fashioned as they are added to the shape of a rose. Twist the base of the petals and add stem wire. Wrap stem wire with green tissue. Curl the edges of the outer petals.

Canterbury Bell

Fold a piece of blue tissue 8" × 2" in half to make 4" × 2". Cut out shape with aid of template. Roll three thin strips of yellow tissue, each four inches long, tightly to make three stamens. Open out the blue tissue, place stamens in position and fashion a bell by wrapping the tissue lightly round your thumb and twisting the base together. Alternatively, use the end of a broomstick to get the bell shape. Straighten out the stamens and flatten these at the top. Curl the edges of the bell. Cut five white petals for the calyx. Paste these around the base of the bell after stem wire has been added. Finish with green tissue strip over stem wire.

Poppy

Cut five red petals with the aid of the template. Cut one large centre from white tissue. Cut one small centre from card and cover it with black tissue, twisting the tissue on the reverse side to form a small stem (see diagram). Push this stem through the middle of the large centre piece, arrange the petals in poppy shape. Twist the base of the petals around the black stem. Add stem wire and cut away any surplus black tissue. Wrap stem with green tissue strip.

African Daisy

This attractive little flower can be made in a number of different colours. Make a template with ruler and compass as indicated in the diagram. Cut about four pieces of tissue paper, say of purple, each large enough to take the template shape. Put tissue and template together and cut out flower shape. Cut a small centre piece of card, as for the poppy, but cover it with yellow tissue, twisting the surplus to form a small stem. Paste the flower shapes together at their centre, then make a small hole in this centre and thread through the yellow stem of the centre piece and fasten this in position with paste. Wrap stem wire round the yellow stem and finish with green tissue.

Leaves

These can be made in various ways from different shades of green or other colours. They can be first cut from thin card and the card then covered with tissue, or they can be from single or double thicknesses of tissue. They can be easily copied from the real thing or from pictures in books, or you can invent shapes.

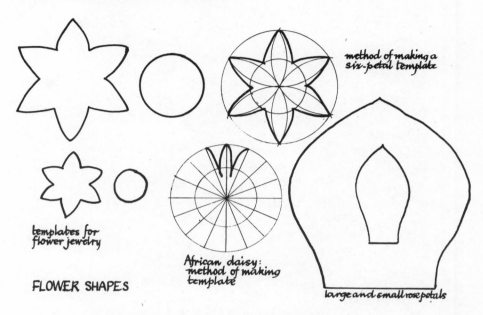

method of making a six-petal template

templates for flower jewelry

FLOWER SHAPES

African daisy: method of making template

large and small rose petals

6. Flower shapes (2) including templates for jewellery

Flower Jewellery

Tissue paper, card, preferably of the colour of the tissue you are using but white will do, thin paste and some means of attachment are required for these.

The card is first cut to the desired shape. Tissue of one colour is then cut to the shape of the card but a little larger so that the edges may be pasted down on the reverse side of the card.

Paste on six layers of tissue paper over the card, folding over the edges of the tissue on to the reverse side and finishing off this side neatly with more tissue of the same colour. Let the paste dry out until it reaches the stage where you can press and mould the petals with your fingers, so that when thoroughly dry the flower keeps the required shape.

When you have shaped the flower, let it dry thoroughly. It will dry hard, and a centre-piece may be added.

33

9. Flower jewellery: made from card covered with tissue paper, showing brooch, pendant, necklace and bracelet

10. Mounted flower piece: showing individual flowers mounted as a form of collage

A centre-piece may be made by pasting yellow tissue paper on card. Centres of material other than tissue and card can be used, for example, foam rubber, velvet or other raised cloth. A little tube glue should be used to fasten the centre-piece.

Pendants, brooches, bracelets and necklaces can all be made this way by varying the size of the flowers. Silk cord or ribbon can be used for stringing purposes.

The finished flowers can be lacquered: clear nail varnish will do for small pieces.

For a brooch pin, a suitable safety pin is fastened to the back of the flower with a piece of adhesive plaster.

Mounted Flower Pieces

These are a form of collage. According to what you wish to achieve, the flowers are mounted on card.

Card of a suitable colour should be used for the work.

For a basket of flowers arranged as a collage, take a large piece of coloured card and on this, in the form of a basket, arrange a piece of card of another colour. To get the basket shape, experiment with newspaper until you get the shape you want, then trace round this on to the basket card. Leave tabs on this card which can be folded under. When fixing the basket in position, do it by gluing down these tabs: this will raise the basket up a little.

The flowers to fill the basket are made like the independent flowers already described, but without the stem being added. Also, any surplus tissue at the base is cut away.

Make a number of flowers of various bright colours, and before pasting them into position, arrange them in the basket as attractively as you can. When the result satisfies you, use a white paste to fix them in place. Leaves can likewise be added.

Boxes can be decorated with small, tissue paper flowers, arranged and pasted into a pattern on the lid and sides. Cylindrical boxes are particularly suited for this form of decoration. The box should first be covered with a tinted paper.

6. USE OF TISSUE PAPER WITH WAXED PAPER

Unusual and interesting decorations can be made using tissue and waxed paper. Small cut-outs placed between two sheets of waxed paper can form a unit for a wall hanging. Windows can be decorated for festive occasions, such as Christmas-time, with tissue figures laid between sheets of waxed paper. Other decorative uses, such as lampshades and hangings, a decoration for a glass door, and so on, may suggest themselves to you as you experiment with the two papers.

Waxed paper can generally be obtained in rolls at stationers.

Window Decoration

Let us suppose that we have a window with four separate panes of glass of the same size. Measure and cut eight pieces of waxed paper to fit the panes.

Cut a circle template about four inches in diameter from card. A lid or the bottom of a round tin will serve in lieu of a compass.

Take three or four different colours of tissue and with the aid of the template cut a number of circles of tissue paper. A small cut-out is now made from each circle. Refer to the diagram for circular cut-outs.

Fold each circle across the diameter, then three times across the radius making four folds in all. Then cut pieces out of the folded circle, and open it. Vary the cuts for each circle and some interesting shapes will result.

Place a piece of the waxed paper on top of several sheets of newspaper in front of you. Arrange the cut-outs on this to make a satisfactory pattern: about six circles should do, but the size of the window-pane is the governing factor. Place another piece of waxed paper over the tissue cut-outs, taking care not to disturb them. The two pieces of waxed paper are then sealed by going over them with a hot iron.

The decoration for one pane is now ready. The corners of the waxed paper can be attached to the glass with a little white paste. The process

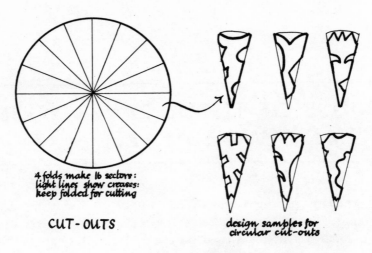

CUT-OUTS

4 folds make 16 sectors: light lines show creases: keep folded for cutting

design samples for circular cut-outs

7. Circular cut-outs

is repeated for the remaining panes.

For the decoration of a glass door panel, flower cut-outs can be used between waxed paper.

Wall Hangings

For a wall hanging, take two lengths of waxed paper. Measure one length into sections and in each section place a few tissue cut-outs. Alternating patterns are effective, and each section can be separated with a thin strip of dark tissue.

When the sections are complete, place the other piece of waxed paper over them and seal with a hot iron. Remember to have some sheets of newspaper under the waxed paper when ironing.

To finish for hanging fasten a piece of dowel at each end, and tie a piece of yarn or string to the top dowel.

Similar wall hangings can be made by using long strips of tissue paper about an inch and a half wide lengthwise in the waxed paper. Effective combinations can be made, such as purple and black strips, royal blue and white strips, bright red and yellow strips. When arranging the strips, separate them slightly. The strength of the colour can be increased by putting two or more thicknesses of tissue.

7. SIMPLE MODELS

One of the easiest yet most decorative models is the fish. It lends itself to many variations of technique.

To start with, thin reed is best for the shape, but failing this soft wire or a frame cut from card can be used.

Take a piece of reed about three feet long and bend it round so that the ends cross. Let about seven inches of reed protrude on each side, and fasten the reed, where it crosses, with a little light thread. A glance at the photograph will show what is meant.

This makes a simple, stylized fish shape.

Cover the shape with tissue paper. The tissue can be cut larger than the shape; the shape is given a thin layer of white paste and the tissue is laid on this. When the tissue is fast, trim away the surplus paper.

Variations of surface on the fish shape can be achieved by adding more tissue in different ways. For example, small circles of coloured tissue to imitate scales are applied singly over the first covering of tissue paper. Begin pasting on the scales from the tail end, and overlap them as you go. Do not paste the whole of the tissue circle down: leave the part that is uncovered, when you overlap it, free so that the finished scales are raised.

Other fish shapes can be made from reed by tying or gluing more reed to the simple shape: crosspieces can be added to separate the head and to provide supports for ventral and dorsal fins.

More complicated fish shapes from reed can be made as follows. Draw the shape of the fish you want on a piece of board or plywood. Around and on this outline knock in a number of half-inch nails. Give the reed a good soaking in water and, when it is pliable enough, wrap it carefully round the outline made by the nails. Let the reed dry, and when it is dry it should retain the shape of the outline.

Tissue patterned with potato prints can be used for covering shapes.

For a stronger model, first cover the shape with card as a base to cover. A raised texture can be given to this by covering it with tissue as

39

for the raised collages. Try a rainbow of colours for this.

On the same principle of tissue paper over a reed outline, many other simple models are possible. Some suggestions are shields, flat masks and butterflies.

Butterflies are interesting to make. Like the fish, the form is stylized, made as the fancy takes you but in essence keeping to the shape of the butterfly. The body can be of any suitable material, and the antennae and legs of reed.

11. Simple models: butterfly and fish from reed and tissue paper

Cork is probably best for the body. Corks can be saved from wine bottles and glued together to the size required: a piece of wire pushed through the corks helps to keep them in place. Wings, legs and antennae can be pushed into the cork, but first prepare a hole for the reed with a bradawl, and put a touch of glue on the tip of the reed before you push it into the hole. The shape can, of course, be assembled before you do any gluing, in order to make sure that you have the shape correctly.

Dragon-flies are another form of model made like butterflies. Shapes should always be painted an appropriate colour before the tissue is added.

8. CONSTRUCTIONS

By a construction I mean a decorative piece of work which is quite un-like a known shape. Of course, geometrical figures will come into the making of a construction, but the final shape should be something unique. It is simply a play of fancy.

For our purpose, it must be decorative, and this sets limits to our fancy. Other limits are imposed by our medium, in this instance tissue paper.

Nevertheless our constructions can take on a variety of forms and provide much scope for creative work.

A first requirement is a base sufficiently heavy to hold the construction without fear of its overbalancing, yet unobtrusive. Since tissue is so light, soft wood, such as deal, will do very well.

A preliminary sketch can be made; although this is not absolutely necessary, it does afford a guide, and can always be altered as the work proceeds.

Having decided on the form the construction is to take, prepare the base by sandpapering and rounding the edges.

Some lengths of reed are cut, and holes are bored in the base, according to your sketch, to receive the ends of the reed. The ends can be pointed slightly.

Arrange the reed in the base: they will represent the lines in your drawing. When the arrangement is satisfactory—the lengths can be altered at will—fasten the ends in the base with a touch of glue.

When the glue is dry, the base and the reed can be painted or stained and varnished, if desired.

The shapes made by the reed are now covered with tissue paper. Put a thin layer of white paste over the reed and the tissue can be laid on this. If you put on the tissue larger than the shape it can always be trimmed down when the paste is dry.

Both sides of the shape may be covered. Light tissue can be overlaid with strips of dark tissue, or with small, geometrical shapes. These con-

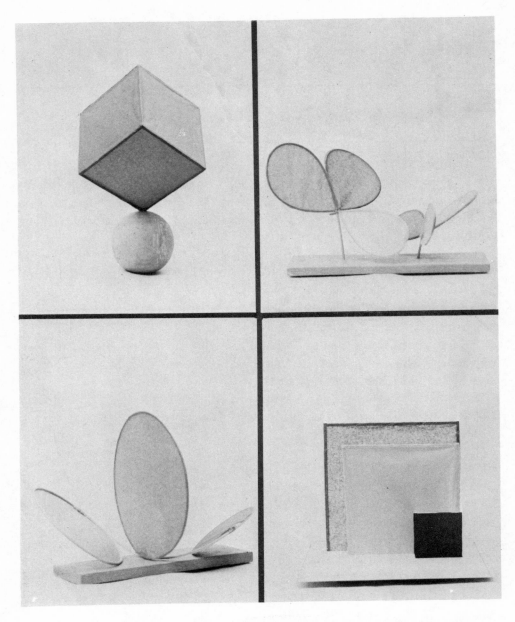

12. Four types of construction, very easily made but effective as decoration

structions are most effective if stood in positions where light may penetrate them. A diffused light behind a construction enhances the decoration.

Other types of construction can be made by using thin strips of wood or dowel instead of reed.

For example, cut six lengths of thin dowel of three different lengths. Drill holes in a base to fit the dowel. Arrange the dowel in the base to form three pairs of uprights of different sizes. Three squares of tissue paper of different colours are fastened to these uprights with white paste. The tissue can be patterned with potato prints.

Using only two uprights, you can attach strips of tissue to form a warp, and pass other strips through them vertically to make the weft.

Thin wire twisted to form a number of simple, closed two-dimensional shapes can be wound with strips of tissue, and the shapes covered with other tissue. This is done before pushing the ends of the wire into a base.

All the above are put forward as ideas which may be improved upon. Even if you do not make a drawing and are a bit uncertain about what you want to make, the thing is to make a start and let the construction grow. The essential here is to get started: you will be agreeably surprised to see how the creative part of you takes over.

There is no need to confine yourself to reed or wire for the basic shapes—although reed and tissue go so well together that they might have been made for each other—you can use balsa wood, card, thin metal, plastic and so on.

9. MOBILES

Attractive mobiles can be made with reed and tissue paper.

Cut some lengths of reed about four feet long. Bend the reed to make a figure eight. Do not try to flatten the reed but let it take its own shape. Fasten the centre of the figure with thread.

Tissue paper is then glued to the reed to cover the enclosed spaces. This makes a basic unit for a mobile. These units can be made with three parts, rather like a clover leaf, or of four parts, like a four-leaf clover. The size of the enclosed spaces should vary.

Part of the beauty of this mobile comes from the different curved shapes assumed by the reed when you bend it.

Thin binding wire is ideal for hanging purposes. Thread can be used to suspend the units from the wire.

Since these mobiles are very light in weight, they should not be hung where there is a strong current of wind. A light breeze is sufficient to cause them to turn. If by any chance they are too light, then a small weight, such as a piece of lead, can be attached unobtrusively to the centre of the units to create a steady balance.

Colour schemes can be worked out with these mobiles, the reeds being covered with a number of different colours. Other pleasant alternatives are to pattern the tissue with potato prints before attaching it to the reed: the same pattern can be used for different parts of the units. Or the prepared units can be overlaid with more tissue in strips of another colour.

Small fish shapes (see under the heading of 'Simple Models') can be hung as a mobile.

Another interesting form of mobile is made with small circles of reed and tissue paper. On each unit a face or pattern is made with tissue paper or coloured yarn. A number of these units are suspended on a single thread, and three or four threads make up the mobile. The threads are attached to a short length of dowel or a disc of hardboard. They should be of different lengths and the units spaced to prevent

13. Mobiles made from reed and tissue paper

their knocking one against the other.

Similar mobiles can be made with triangular or other geometrical units. A small weight, such as a large bead, at the end of the thread helps to steady the mobile. Very suitable weights can be made from clay and painted.

45

14. A mobile made from small circles of reed decorated with tissue paper. Waxed paper with tissue paper: small circular cut-outs pressed between two sheets of waxed paper to form a wall hanging

46

10. MOULDED OBJECTS FROM READY-MADE MOULDS

The next two headings deal with yet another way of working with tissue paper and thin paste. This is in the creation of three-dimensional objects, such as bowls, vases, masks and puppet heads.

The way to acquire a little skill in this is to start with modelling over a ready-made object, such as a glass. Let it be a plain glass, a half-pint beer glass, for example, with straight sides.

Cover the outside of the glass with a thin coat of vaseline.

Cut or tear some inch squares of white tissue and one other colour.

Put a layer of white tissue squares over the vaseline, overlapping each square as you go and using more vaseline to fasten down the tissue if necessary.

It will facilitate the work if you place the glass upside down over the neck of a bottle or something similar. Let the tissue come below the rim of the glass.

Now paste on alternate layers of white and coloured tissue, taking care to overlap the tissue and to smooth each layer well down with paste. The reason for using white and a coloured tissue is to make it easier to check on an even coverage.

About six layers should be sufficient.

Let the paste dry out, then trim round the rim of the glass and remove the tissue paper shape from the glass. It will slip off easily, because of the vaseline.

Seal the edges of the object with two more layers of tissue paper. Let this dry and it is ready for painting.

It will be seen that vases and bowls can be made in the same way. Allow more layers for a larger object.

Objects with undercuts are a little more difficult to model, as they present a problem when it comes to removing the shape from the mould. The removal of a tissue shape from a mould with undercuts can usually

47

be done in one of two ways. One is to cut the shape evenly in two lengthwise: the puppet head (under the next heading) is an example of this. The other is to cut round it horizontally by the undercut. In both instances, the two resulting parts of the shape must be fastened together again.

Fasten the halves by coating the two cut edges with a thin layer of glue, and press them together. Then go over the join with two layers of tissue paper and paste.

Modelling over Balloons

A balloon makes an excellent base for creating shapes from tissue paper.

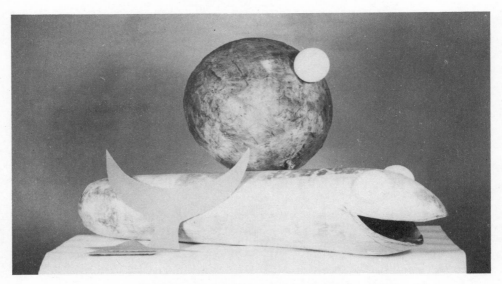

15. Modelling over balloons: clown's head and fish

Inflate the balloon and secure the opening. Paste several large squares of tissue paper over the balloon, overlapping them as you work and making sure that the tissue is applied evenly all over. Two colours of tissue, a different one for each alternating layer, is helpful here.

About eight layers of tissue paper should suffice to give a firm foundation to work on.

Let it dry. From this shape, you can create masks, fish, giant insects, spiders, lanterns and other objects.

16. Finished clown's head together with small figure modelled first over plasticine
then taken from the mould

Modelling over Waste Articles

Plastic bottles, jars, small cartons and other containers, which are normally thrown away, can be the base for a number of tissue paper models.

Vases can be made from suitable plastic containers. First trim the top from the container. The bottom will need to be weighted, in order to keep it upright when in use. This can be done by mixing a little plaster and pouring it into the bottom of the container. When the plaster is dry it will knock out easily. Take it out and glue it back into position.

Cover the container with tissue paper squares and paste. When this is dry, it can be left as it is and varnished, or a design or pattern can be drawn on it and painted and varnished. The varnish helps to prevent water spoiling it.

11. MOULDED OBJECTS FROM OWN MOULDS

The more interesting form of modelling over a mould, and the more creative, is when you make your own moulds.

Clay or plasticine is used to make the moulds.

Potter's clay is easiest to work with, but it is normally good for only one type of object, since it dries hard. It can be used any number of times for the same object. The clay may crack as it dries, and the cracks have to be made good with other clay.

However, clay can be used again, if you care to take the trouble of crushing the clay to powder and mixing this powder with water to form a liquid. Let the liquid settle. The clay will fall to the bottom of the container. Pour off the water through a fine sieve, and let the clay

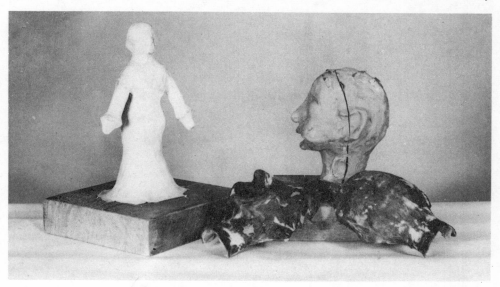

17. Modelling over own moulds: small figure made over plasticine mould. Puppet head, showing method of removing model from the mould

method of pasting on paper squares: first layer of Vaseline and paper squares only
PUPPET HEAD

8. Method of pasting tissue paper on plasticine model

18. Finished puppet head and two Japanese masks (unfinished) made over clay moulds and copied from photographs

dry out sufficiently to enable it to be used again.

Plasticine can be used several times, provided it is kept clean. Hard plasticine can be softened by letting it stand in warm water for a while.

To avoid having to use too much plasticine on large moulds a form of armature can be made first and the plasticine laid on over this. The armature can take the form of a piece of wood, or a padding of newspaper. To lay plasticine over an armature, roll it into a ball and then flatten it out. The flat pieces are easily put over an armature and fashioned into shape.

Durable puppet heads and masks can be made with tissue paper and paste. Eight layers will form a really hard shell.

After you have prepared your mould, proceed as described for modelling over ready-made moulds.

First apply a coating of vaseline, then apply layers of tissue squares and paste.

Since most of your own moulds are likely to have undercuts, it will be necessary to cut the tissue shape evenly in two in order to remove it from the mould. The two pieces are then rejoined with a thin layer of glue around the cut edges, and the glued join is reinforced with some more tissue and paste.

Piñatas

These are a happy, festive form of decoration which are used at children's parties in Mexico, and are increasing in popularity in those regions of the U.S.A. bordering Mexico.

They consist of a hollow clay or papier mâché container which holds sweets, and over which is modelled in card the shape of an animal or other form. The whole thing is then covered with tissue paper in frills.

It always adds fun and gaiety, and at a given moment at a party, the piñata is broken and the children scramble for the sweets.

There is more than one way of achieving the frilled effect of a piñata decoration. A simple method is as follows.

Cut several lengths of tissue paper three inches wide and fold lengthwise. Cut across the fold at intervals of about a quarter of an inch and an inch or more deep along the whole length.

According to the part of the shape being covered, this frilled tissue is cut to size and pasted on. Always start at the bottom of an object and work up, hiding the pasted part of the previous frill and leaving the frill exposed.

Three or four lengths of tissue can be cut, folded and frilled at the

19. Making piñatas

20. Finished piñatas hung as a mobile

same time, if desired. But care should be taken when separating them to avoid tearing.

The photograph will help to make the above clearer.

A papier mâché container can be readily made over a balloon: use damp newspaper and paste for this. When dry, part of the container can be cut away neatly with a sharp knife, the sweets put in, and the part pasted back into place again.

These can of course be made simply as an attractive form of decoration.

12. SCROLLS

These are based on the Japanese type of wall scroll. The size is a matter of choice.

For the bottom end piece a length of three quarter of an inch dowel is used: it should protrude on each side of the scroll for about an inch. It is sandpapered smooth and painted black.

The top piece is a piece of dowel or lath the same length as the width of the cloth. A piece of cord is attached to this for hanging.

A piece of thin material, say 42" × 12", is hemmed top and bottom, the hems being large enough to take the dowel pieces. These can be measured by wrapping the material around the dowel before hemming. The sides of the material can also receive a narrow hem.

A piece of tissue paper, say 28" × 8½", is then prepared. It will probably be necessary to make this size from two pieces of tissue paper, pasting one to the other as neatly as possible.

A print or drawing is made on the tissue paper and this is then mounted on the material by a thin smear of white paste around the edge of the tissue. The position of the tissue paper on the material should be marked out beforehand, and this can be done with a thin line of white chalk.

The design on the tissue paper can be based on primitive art. Many designs can be adapted for this sort of work. The simpler and more bold the design, the better the effect.

First a preliminary sketch is made and details either altered or omitted as thought fit. A full-size drawing is then made in charcoal on drawing paper: failing drawing paper, newspaper will do. The tissue paper is laid over this drawing and lightly rubbed all over: do not move the tissue when doing this. The design is thus transferred to the tissue. Blow away any surplus charcoal and the tissue is ready for printing.

Suitable vegetables may be cut for the printing. These are charged with paint and used over the design on the tissue. Or a felt pen will give a good line effect.

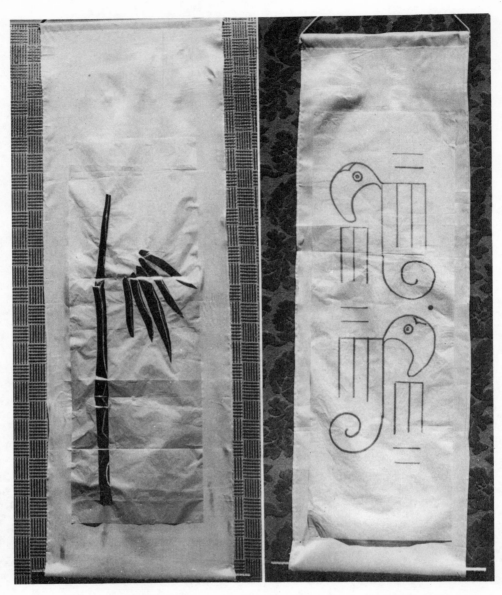

21. Scrolls: metallic paper on tissue, and a design drawn on with a felt pen

When the design is finished and dry it is mounted on the material. These designs can be changed from time to time. To remove an old design from the material dampen the edges of the tissue paper where it is fastened. Let the moisture soak in and the paper can be lifted or scraped away easily.

Cut-outs from metallic paper can also be used on tissue paper for scroll work. The design is first made on drawing paper and then traced on to the metallic paper for cutting out.

Work under the headings of 'Cut-outs', 'Prints' and 'Collages' can also be mounted in this attractive manner.

There are some excellent books for reference from which many ideas for patterns and designs can be obtained. These are:

The Book of Signs by Rudolf Koch

Decorative Art of the Southwestern Indians by Dorothy Smith Sides

Hornung's Handbook of Designs and Devices

Design Motifs of Ancient Mexico by Jorge Encisco

The above are all Dover paperbacks and are published by Dover Publications Inc., New York, U.S.A. They can most probably be ordered through your local bookseller.

13. OTHER USES FOR TISSUE PAPER

There are many other uses to which tissue paper can be put. A few are set out below.

Party Hats

A basic shape for these is made from a strip of card, the width depending on the type of hat you wish to make. Put the strip of card round the head of the person for whom the hat is being made and mark off the size in pencil. The card is then fastened with staples or Sellotape and any surplus cut away. All kinds of hats can be made on this shape, the tissue paper being modelled over the card strip. Streamers and flowers from tissue can be added as decoration. Brims and peaks are made from card and attached to the basic shape before tissue paper is used. Cones of card can be made into hats by covering them with tissue paper, decorating the top with tissue pompoms or streamers. A thin rubber band may be necessary to keep cone hats in place.

Carnival Mops

Make a thin cylinder of card about eighteen inches long and about about three quarters of an inch in diameter. The shape may be obtained by wrapping the card round a broomstick. Sellotape it securely. Cover it with tissue paper, which may be pasted on, and tuck in and secure the ends. Cut a number of tissue streamers of different colours, about $18'' \times \frac{3}{4}''$, and fasten them in one end of the cylinder. You now have something you can wave at the procession. A variation of this is to make mops of a single colour as a decoration. The card cylinder may also be covered with strips of metallic paper, instead of tissue.

The Use of Tissue Paper with Chicken Wire

The open mesh wire used in chicken runs is ideal for some kinds of tissue paper work. The basic idea is to fill each hole with a small roll of tissue paper, which is then slightly flattened, when it will appear rather like a small rose. The tissue may be rolled around a pencil or a finger and shaped; it should fit the mesh tightly. Many types of decoration can be built up in this way. The wire is first cut to a desired shape and size. For example, shields, emblems, and monograms can be made this way. A carnival float can also be decorated in this manner. The wire mesh is shaped and fitted in place and then patterned with small tissue paper rolls.

Plaited Tissue

Tissue paper can be folded into strips and plaited. These plaits can then be woven to make table mats, or built up into other forms, such as small baskets and containers. Table mats can be pasted on to a cardboard base.

Stained Glass Windows

A stencil design is drawn on to black pastel paper or card. It is then cut out and the spaces covered with tissue paper. Christmas angels look well in this medium. Simple geometrical designs are also effective, while being fairly easy to cut out. Ties must be left between the spaces. Remember that if you cannot draw too well, enlargements of small illustrations are not difficult, following the method shown earlier for enlarging the racing car.